Tamim Al-Barghouti published six poetry collections in both colloquial and classical Arabic, including *Meejana* (1999), *Al-Manzar* "The Scene" (2000), *Maqam Iraq* (2005), *Fil Quds* "In Jersualem" (2008) and *Ya Masr Hanet* (2012), and two academic books on Arab politics and history. He received his PhD in political science from Boston University in 2004, and has since taught at Georgetown University, the Free University in Berlin, and the American University in Cairo. He was also a fellow at the Berlin Institute for Advanced Studies 2007-2008. A columnist since 2003, writing in Egyptian and Lebanese dailies, Al-Barghouti has been associated with the 2011 uprisings, and with political activism in Egypt and Palestine. He is currently based in Beirut and works at the United Nations Economic and Social Commission for West Asia.

IN JERUSALEM
AND OTHER POEMS

IN JERUSALEM

AND OTHER POEMS
1997-2017

BY
TAMIM AL-BARGHOUTI

TRANSLATED BY
RADWA ASHOUR

Interlink Books

An imprint of Interlink Publishing Group, Inc.
Northampton, Massachusetts

First published in 2017 by
Interlink Books
An imprint of
Interlink Publishing Group, Inc.
46 Crosby Street, Northampton, MA 01060
www.interlinkbooks.com

Library of Congress Cataloging-in-Publication Data
Names: Barghūthī, Tamīm author. | ʿĀshūr, Radwá translator. | Soueif,
Ahdaf translator. | Morigan, Pan, 1958- editor.
Title: In Jerusalem: and other poems, 1997-2017 / by Tamim al-Barghouti;
translated by Radwa Ashour and Ahdaf Soueif ; edited by Pan Morigan.
Description: Northampton, MA : Interlink Books, 2017.
Identifiers: LCCN 2017008859 | ISBN 9781566560238
Classification: LCC PJ7916.A788 A6 2017 | DDC 892.7/17--dc23
LC record available at https://lccn.loc.gov/2017008859

Book design by Pam Fontes-May
Edited by Pan Morigan
Cover illustration by Hammam Al-Masri,
based on a photograph by Gary Doak

Printed and bound in the United States of America

*Thanks are due to all who made these translations possible,
especially to the valuable advice on the translation given by
Pan Morigan, Sharif Elmusa, and Ahdaf Soueif*

for Radwa Ashour

Table of Contents

Genesis

Translated by Radwa Ashour

They realized a mouse
Was hiding in some corner
Of their home
So they placed cheese
On a wooden plank coated with glue
The mouse leapt at the cheese
And was stuck to the board
A cat followed the mouse
And was also fixed
A dog came after the cat
Like them, he was caught
A child followed the dog
Mother followed child
After mother came father
A policeman saw what happened
And, attempting a rescue,
Was also trapped
The State Security officer noticed
That the policeman was late
He tried to investigate
So he too was riveted to the board
The State, realizing its Security was absent,
Got scared, and went to look for it
And when the State found its Security
Both were stuck to the plank
The eagle, the State's emblem
Saw that the state had disappeared
Swooping off the flag
It landed upon the crowded board
Taking its place in a long line—

At whose rear stood the State
And at the front
Sat a piece of cheese

Unfortunately
Just then
Saturn and Mars
Crossed one another
Causing a great flood
The board floated away
With all its passengers
Through the pages of
A history book!

God and Goat[1]

Translated by Tamim Al-Barghouti

Omar Ibn Al-Khattab, the Caliph known for his legendary sense of justice, once said: if I heard, in Medina, that a goat stumbled in Iraq, I would be unable to sleep, for the guilt of having failed to level the road for her!

A goat is stumbling in the rubble
Searching the remains
Of the Baghdad National Museum
For a leaf or a document

To a hungry goat, they make no difference,
Nor do they differ one from the other in reality

A leaf in the rubble documents it
A document brings the rubble to life

Maybe the goat knows better
Let the roads be leveled for her.

It is said that Nebu, god of wisdom in Ancient Babylon, fell in love with a goat. He tried to capture her. Frightened, she fled. What could the god of wisdom want? She didn't understand. Even if she had, would the god give her little goats? Would he fight the other rams for her? When he grew old, would he relinquish her to the

---

1. This poem is from my collection, Maqam Iraq (Cairo, 2005,) which draws on traditional Iraqi forms alternating between folk and classical poetry, and prose narratives. The book consists of seven sections, each revolving around a central figure or object which, in the Arab imagination, is associated with Iraq. The excerpt below is a translation of my own along with some changes introduced to the original Arabic text, rendering it comprehensible to non-Arabic speaking readers.

strongest ram in the herd? The goat didn't want the god, yet the god wanted the goat! And the council of gods was in disarray.

Enlil: What a scandal! What a disgrace! That crazy brother of ours will be the end of us all. We are the Ones seen only in dreams. We are the ones approached with fear, even in imagination! Yet, each and every night, we must collect our brother from doorsteps and backyards, chasing a goat! And hear those yellow-toothed peasants joking. Oh, what shall we do with him? A god chasing a goat! Where is his self-esteem, his authority, his divinity?

Anu: Don't talk about divinity, dear brother... If not for the people's kind hearts, we would not exist. We are their hopes and fears. We are theirs, they are not ours. You know what divinity is about, brother. We are nothing....

Enlil: Watch your words! We make the seas flow, the winds blow, and plants grow in a rock's heart. We command the fire in the cloud and the rain in lightening, and you say we're nothing. What's the matter with you?

Anu: Brother, you know better, the seas flow, the winds blow, and plants grow in the hearts of rocks. And you cannot even fix your own breakfast! We are nothing.

Enlil: You're wrong, I swear by their bowed heads and open palms, we are the people's hope. We are their theory, their guess. Do you know what a guess can do? A guess is what blows the winds and moves the waves. Nothing fills the space between the brown rug and the blue tent. But that 'nothing' is what keeps it from crashing down on the heads of men. We are the air that holds the water that holds the land that holds the sons of men... brother!

Anu: A bubble!

Enlil: Fine, a bubble named the world, my friend. And that crazy brother of yours is placing it on a goat's horn! A speechless mix of hair and dust!

Anu: We are nothing while the goat is something. She is right in rejecting our brother the professor. The goat is of a higher rank than us. We're a guess, we are names, language. Does language bite? If you put language in a field of barley, will you have less barley the next day? Tell me, Enlil, have you ever protected your worshipers from a flood? Have you offered them water in times of drought? Have you granted them victory against an overwhelming enemy? Have you planted love in the heart of a poet's beloved, when the poet was about to commit suicide because she was in love, not with him, but with the garbage man instead? Tell me Enlil, have you done anything besides handing out names like sweets at weddings or black coffee at mourning services? You called the flood your wrath, the drought a war between us two, the girl's rejection a sin for which she must burn at your altar and the poet a martyr, over whose shrine a temple should be erected—to you! You're just handing out names Enlil! We are but names and name givers, good brother. If it weren't for names we'd be mere statues—unemployed granite. Yet a goat is a goat, call her a parrot, a monkey, a wave, a dream, a crisis, a blessing, a curse, an offering. I swear that wouldn't change the sound of her bleating, or the movement of her jaws as she gnaws on grass. It would not change her bad smell or her lust for rams. The goat is a goat whatever you call her. The goat is of a higher rank than us!

Enlil: You're a god who knows not what he says. We might be a metaphor but we're not a lie. We're images but we're not idols. We're silent but we're not meaningless. Think of the priests at Ur and Lagash. What would happen to them without us! Think of the woman who believes that her son, who never grew older than ten,

became a young palm tree in your temple! What would happen to the men who fought the war and lost, fasting so you'd help them win the next? What would happen to those who fought and won only for your sake? What happens to the besieged, when all roads to their city are blocked, except the one leading to the stars...
We are the geometry in palace walls, the seasons in fields of grain. We might not exist, but without us, the world would crumble.

Anu: It is already crumbling, my brother. Can't you see the wreckage?

Enlil: Through us, the spell can be reversed. The roads will be leveled, the temples built. The defeated will rise and the victors fall. After all, this is what gods do.

Anu: Our job is a crime

Enlil: A perpetual, kind and glorious crime. A crime insisted upon is a crime forgiven... Love your crime and it will be your message. A sin only becomes so when you regret it. If you embrace it, it becomes your creed. A crime insisted upon is law itself, a crime insisted upon is a crime no more. Be patient brother, the tapestry of history is unfinished. We have a job to do!

Anu: Why wait? History is an epic written on an hourglass. You read it once upright and once upside down, and you cannot tell the difference. Why wait? Your brother is already chasing a goat through piles of garbage. No wonder he is the god of wisdom. It was not love that struck him when he opened his eyes. It was knowledge; wisdom of the ignorant, sight of the blind, the type of knowledge denied to gods. He knew of the besieged, the triumphant, the defeated. You saw their piety; he saw their blasphemy. You saw their fear. He saw their anger. Will you have us wait for the people to stone us? On that day you'd wish to be a goat!

Enlil (disgusted): Me, wish to be a goat?

Anu: You think a goat beneath you? Fine, can you be a goat?

Enlil: I am a god!

Anu: Answer me, can you be a goat, a lion, a cow, a donkey, a plow, a lock, a key, a pair of shoes. Enlil, can you *be*?!

Enlil: I told you, I. *am*. A god.

At this point, we're told, Anu left the council of the gods. When people from UNESCO searched the ruins of the Museum, they found no statues of him. However, some of the missing statues reappeared later in museums beyond the sea. Anu had given up.

Enlil's statues were not found either, though he'd chosen to remain.

Aware that he was still operating somewhere in Iraq, the occupation forces searched every house, looking for him.

The goat kept stumbling about amidst the wreckage.

And Omar, awake all night, alone, was still trying to level the roads.

The Cloud and the Mountain

Translated by Tamim Al-Barghouti

A mountain said to a cloud
"Carry me cloud, carry me please!"

Like a child lifting two hands
Asking his mother to carry him
Like an imam at the end of prayers
Stretching his body skyward
Arms entreating heaven
"Come closer, listen a second!"

As if the mountain were a wave
That batters the fortress walls at Acre
To reach the top
And never gives up

As if the mountain were a boy's voice
That rings out in the midst of a march
Eager to know if his cry makes a difference
He raises his voice, higher, and higher
Trying in vain to hear it

As if the mountain were a grandfather and a baby
All at once
Serious, but kind

As if its rocks were stuffed full of fresh almonds

A mountain said to a cloud—
"Take me with you
Carry me, please"

This cloud was just a child
Tiny, she was
In fact, pathetic
Hammered by the winds of the north and south

A weak cloud like this one
Isn't allowed to go to work
Lest she wither!
A cloud like this one shouldn't even rain!
A resident of deserts
Completely inexperienced—
(Unlike other clouds that travel and visit
Caves of demons and kingdoms of men)

Quite soon, it was said
She'd be fired

They'd let her evaporate away...

Nonetheless, as she was floating by
Minding her problems
The mountain called to her
"Carry me cloud, please carry me"

"What shall I do"
The cloud said to herself
"This mountain is ancient"
(A friend of her father's,
She'd grown up riding his shoulders)

"Had he forgotten who he was?
Or who I was?" She mused,

"Had the laws and customs slipped his mind?
Does the passage of years do this to us?
This is no time for the senile!
Senile?
Or wise?
What do you know?"

How can a cloud ever carry a mountain?!

"Carry me cloud, carry me..."

A mixture of love and pain pierced her
"When did you become so calculating?"
She looked at the mountain and thought:
"What difference will it make?"

She said to him:

"Anything you want, Uncle,

Anything you want!"

In the Arab World, Live

Translated by Tamim Al-Barghouti

In the Arab world, live
Like a cat that lives under a car
Shoes are all you see of life

In the Arab world, live
Like a circus clown
A clown stands on your head
You stand on the next clown's head
And everyone stands with utmost respect
Serious and very well dressed

In the Arab world, live
Through a football match
That has been going on for a thousand years
Players dash here and there
And the ball always remains
In the hands of the referee

In the Arab world, live
To tell a girl you love her
And, if she loves you back
she'll slap you in the face

In the Arab world, live
To curse the taste of water, falafel,
The coffee-shop and its customers
Your wife and her children
The crowd and the heat in the bus
The tricks of Satan
Being broke

And when you're asked about all that
You say:
"We thank God
May He keep showering us with His blessings"

In the Arab world, live
Like a school boy
Who has to salute the flag in the school yard every morning
While longing for the street outside

In the Arab world, live
Like a hesitant tear in the eyes of the proud
Pain exiles you
Dignity holds you back

In the Arab world live
Watching the time
Lest you miss the news on TV

Only to see
How people
In the Arab world, die.

The Ant

Translated by Radwa Ashour

I am an ant
Trapped in soap foam
Kicking and flailing
"To be or not to be"
Nothing to hold on to
No ground to stand on
I scream and no one hears me
Like a silent consonant in a foreign language
Just an ant trapped in soap foam

The foam swells around me
Like some jinni from a lamp
Stretching his back and yawning
With one foot splayed before me
Head high as heaven

He peers at me with contempt
And I am an ant with dignity
I thought if I yelled at him
A miracle might unfold
God might shrink him
Stuff him back into that lamp

No such luck...
I remained an ant in soap foam

The foam swells, becomes an Independence Square
Of foam, government buildings rise
Crowds queue in the corridors
Traffic jams

Car horns make a symphony
At night, florescent coke ads
Along with "the intellectual"
do "the enlightenment!"
All power flows to the color gray
"Freely elected by the people"
(Inspect their hands and feet with care
You'll see the nail holes)

Hear me Square!
Dull as a composition lesson
Dangerous as a butcher's blade
Hanging overhead
We don't matter after all
I am just an ant
And you are soap-foam

And now the foam swells
Becomes Arab lands
A Quran in a martyr's hand
A Quran made into a golden necklace
A land of wonders
Where defeat is a necessary item of furniture in every home
Like curtains and sofas
A nation of foam
Whose sorrows are forged of iron
Like palace gates
Where death is a wandering drummer
Passing our windows each dawn

"Wake up now
Or sleep forever!"

My nation—home of longing
You haunt me
You're no big deal, and neither am I
After all
I am just an ant and you are soap-foam

The foam flows on, becoming the universe
Ride the satellite and see
An orbiting problem!
We're all stuck with it
Every escape route leads back
To where you started
A planet, alone in the void
A kidnapped child

Now ditch your satellite and look around
See the clown perched on a throne
His face painted in seven colors
He's playing king
Issuing commands

You laugh
Surely he jests
Soon drowning in blood, you realize
The joke's on you

You'll see, hope aches
Like rheumatism in old bones
A sea
You thirst you drink
You drink you thirst

Oh, Circus!
Dubbed 'The World'
You're no big deal
Nor am I
After all I'm just an ant
And you are soap foam

And the foam grows, becoming death
Welcome oh merciful one
Save me from this net
I'll be so grateful
Don't worry
I seek no revenge, no blood money
After all I am just an ant
And you
Even you
Are only soap foam

Gift

Translated by Radwa Ashour

My life is a gift
Given to me
On my zero birthday
Today I pulled the ribbon
Unwrapped the box
And found many things
Ordinary, yet wonderful
A watch of gold

And of gold
Each hour of life

I received a jack-in-the box
Which makes me laugh—
or scares me to death, it depends,
And two beautiful dolls
The first is a toy
The second is not

Next came a prisoner's crown
And the shackles of a king
I also found a Jack of Spades
Turned him upside down
And he stayed the same

Deep in the box
I found books
And a video, hours-long
Labeled fifty years of conflict
Between the Zionists and the Arabs

I found hell in an inkpot
And heaven in an inkpot too
I found an Arab horse on a race-track
Covered with glue
I found a stove with no flames.
And at the very bottom of the box
I found a white card with my name on it

The rest has not been written

I didn't know what to do with all this stuff!
Oh, God, thank you
But why the trouble?
I put everything back in the box
I closed it up
Wrapped it tight
Tied the ribbon
Threw it skywards and up it went

The gift turned into a host of flying doves
That I will follow forever and ever

Why did I do that?
I really do not know

A Game of Chess

Translated by Radwa Ashour

The black King on the chessboard was worried
The field before him
Whirled with smoke, spears, and swords
His army was exposed
His black pawns quaked
With terror

He shifted his turban
Brushed the dust from his gown
He had sent his men to defend himself
Everywhere
To his right and left
Pawns, bishops, knights
The one remaining Castle
Even the Queen

For a while he was serene
Their deaths posed no problem at all
They die to save his life

But, when the military situation worsened
He suddenly remembered
That if all his pawns perished
He, with no guards, a lonely king
Would surely be defeated
The black King scratched his beard and pondered

The white King was also worried
He was chic and soigné

The dust had not yet reached him
Still, good fortune was not his friend
He often lost his battles
And the black king had all the luck

True, the white pawns were on the offensive
But they were scattered

Life is not always sweet
An enemy might be near defeat
Yet the calamity claims not him—but you

The white King lost his nerve
The black King saw death at his own doorstep
Through a gap between two pawns
The kings stared at one another
In a moment, their eyes met
Over the dead strewn across the board

One king made an offer
Which the other accepted
And this, my friend, was the text of the proposal

"Greetings,
your valiant Majesty
I propose we end this conflict
For as you well know
This game won't end
Until one of us kings dies

But, if the chessmen on both sides
Were to die
You and I may yet live
and the game will end in a draw

Therefore, venerable friend
I propose that you send your men
To squares where they can be killed
And I do the same

Better still, we could both, under oath
Swear to end our mutual enmity
And to hell with the army

Finally, we send cordial greetings
To your valiant Majesty"

The humane offer was accepted

And the two gracious kings
Were now quite busy
Being congratulated
For the ceasefire

The two kings became brothers
With new colors, neither white nor black
Each fond of the other
Close neighbors
Celebrating their friendship
In news bulletins

Meanwhile, the dead chessmen
Remained strewn across the battlefield

Holding tight to their secrets.

Airport

Translated by Radwa Ashour

An airport lounge is much like a homeland
A people, with its various sounds and colors
Policemen, gadgets, bars—
A girl in casual wear
Another in black veil
A packed coffee-shop between them
A child crying as he plays
A child playing, never tiring
A sleeping child
Three women
With neon-painted faces
Discussing a matter of great importance
A mother parting from her son
Their souls sway--
Like wet, transparent shirts touched by a breeze
Betraying their innermost being
The sound of stamps
As an officer forcefully thumps passports
As though he were striking the Romans or the Franks
The tumult of excited American tourists

And there I am
Wandering about
With my fountain pen
Blue lines appear on paper
The curve of each character has weight
Each sentence is a form of masonry

A waiter brings coffee or sugar.
To all, this is an airport,

(Except for this waiter)
For him, the airport is home.

Anyway, the poem has grown long

In a short while
Passengers will depart for their destinations
The crowd will shrink
Like a vitamin tablet in water

And I,
I will remain in the lounge
Raise a flag,
All alone

The Raid

Translated by Radwa Ashour

Turn off the light, turn off the light!
Hear the siren!
It's a raid
Rows of moving crescents pass
Those are lines of bowing men
Bent backs rushing to the shelter
Look, witness
People dashing head over heels
People crying, yes sir, yes sir
Though they do not have a commander
Turn off the light. Turn off the light!

Darkness cloaks
Darkness levels
Green and waste
Frenzied eyes stare and roll
Confused faces
Fail to tell
What is true, what is false.
Turn off the light. Turn off the light.

Hurry up, hurry up!
Outrun all others, be the first
Into the shelter
Stick to the one beside you.

An old man coughs
Everybody coughs.

A boy clutches a slice of bread
The one and only slice in the shelter
He eats
Asking none to share.

An entire people is packed into a shelter
Lumped together, yet separate.

They fled their houses. They let them down
So their houses let them down
Turn off the light. Turn off the light.

In a moment
The shelling will start
Their faces become news bulletins
All are restless
Fear performs its rituals
Inside them.

And now a missile heads this way
To the hunter
A host of birds
Is seductive.

How did he see us?
We can't see our own features
We keep silent. We keep still.

There's not a living person to address

Only death
To smell and to touch
And the dead that have no graves
Turn off the light. Turn off the light.

Our betrayed shelter
One sting, to the faithful, is enough
To learn that lesson:

Now, when the drums of death beat
Long and loud
"Hear the siren!
It's a raid!"

We turn on the light

Turn on the light

Whisper

Translated by Radwa Ashour

A whisper echoed in the desert
Saying: come...
I said
Where are you? I can't see you
Tell me, who are you?
She said, come on
How? I asked
She insisted—
come on!
I froze, looking about, hoping to see her

In the desert, desert was all I found.

She sounded again
Young man, why did you stop, come on!

I shouted: You've been driving me crazy since morning
Nothing to say but "Come on"
Enough!
I'm fed up.

She said: Come on

To hell with you and with whoever wants to follow you!
I walked away.
She said
You've arrived!

Nothing Radical: The Prophecy

Translated by Radwa Ashour

Nothing radical
Great cities will fall
The everlasting photographer
Will dim the light of their skyscrapers
Illuminating mice and garbage bags instead
Which will shine like the domes of parliament

Nothing radical
Cracks in the walls will grow like ivy
Like counter-lightning
Striking upwards
From Earth to heaven

Nothing radical
The autumn trees, stripped naked of leaves
Spread branches like arms in a giant protest
The birds, after long deliberation
Decide not to abandon them

Nothing radical
Schoolchildren will no longer stand in rows
To salute the flags of their countries
Rather, the flags will line up to salute the children

Nothing radical
The deer will arm herself
Bridal gowns will be woven of chain mail
And everyone will prepare for the duties of hospitality

Nothing radical
The fly, with striking tenacity
Will settle on Caesar's crown
And from this lofty position
Mimic his every move

Nothing radical
The masters will reduce the wheat rations
First, for their enemies
Then for their allies
Then for their sons
Then the masters will seize one other by the throat
Allies will regret their alliances
Enemies will regret their enmity
And joy will alight on those least expecting it

Nothing radical
A new religion will be born, as usual, between the Euphrates and the Nile
And, as usual, the military rule of David will vanish

Nothing radical
That large drop of honey lighting the west
Will complete its daily descent into the sea
And melt—the sea becoming a little sweeter

Nothing radical
The dove will lie to Noah's fleet
The crow shall issue warnings
Ships will follow their course from ocean to ocean
The deluge has become as routine
As an ode's refrain
As ordinary as survival

Which is why

The animals living under truce upon the ship
Unafraid of the waves
Look one another in the eye
Hyena and deer alike
Longing for solid ground
A chance to resume the chase

Nothing radical
The cloud knows
Exactly how much rain caused the deluge—
So it's the calmest one on the scene

Being a compassionate cloud
It sends message after message
To those who most doubt salvation
To elderly women whose lives depend on news reports
To infants born with clenched fists—
Accused of terrorism

The cloud forms itself
Into white words
On a blue slate:

People
My people,
You shall overcome.

Joy

Translated by Radwa Ashour

I see depression as an old man with a gentle smile
Familiar as the homeless in the streets
He sleeps on my doorstep
In the morning, he smiles at me on my way out or in
He walks with crutches though I see the wings on his back
I used to ask
What stops someone like you, Sir, from flying?
His answer was a weary look

He lives on my doorstep, my fine guest—
like a line of poetry
With broken grammar and a limping meter
Signifying nothing
He gets angry when I analyze him
I say perhaps he'll get up and leave
I goad him deliberately
I go to extremes
But he knows what I'm up to
And acts like my grandfather
Getting closer and warmer
The more I try to upset him.

Depression, though it arouses sympathy
Is part narcissism
The sad one mostly sees himself
And sorrows, like jealous women
Hide their men from other men's sorrows

Your sorrows, coquette-like, want all of you
They build for you a prison

With mirrored walls, saying
Gaze into your own face, Narcissus of beauty and sorrow
Stare and be content
Be charmed by the beauty
Of victimhood

And Narcissus by the river sits...
But don't assume he's alone
There is another in the water
Don't think our hero is the proud boy
Who loves his own face
No, he is the drowning one
Longing to return to himself—a breathing boy

It's time for the poet to know the truth
Narcissus is in the river, not beside it
Narcissus is a drowning child
Don't stare at some riverside illusion
Swim!
There's no one here but you
So forget him, son of my mother
Don't count on his friendship
Don't believe your mirrors
When they reflect the lines of your face
They're the mirror's lines, my friend, not yours

Don't trust your jealous sorrows
When they advise: stay away from others till you're better
Defeat is camped at your door, let it pass

Tell Defeat, I will not stand aside for you
Nor will I look away while you pass

Break your mirrors
Say to the old man at your door
Come in! Come have some tea with me, then go
I don't care if you live or die
See, here's a razor, take it and shave
Take this jacket and this new shirt and go,
You whose name is Sorrow,
And rejoice!
Don't be embarrassed
By God's gift

God willed the brilliant incongruity
Which sees a person broken when they're whole
Whole when they're broken...
And most valiant when wounded

Let the two Narcissi part at the river
The real one and the ghost

Grandfather Sorrow, you're a child despite the white hair
And not much good at walking

So go forth, walk among the people
For that will heal your limp and grey hair

And if they ask your name, say
I have no name today

But tomorrow morning

I will be known as Joy

In Jerusalem

Translated by Radwa Ashour and Ahdaf Souief

We passed by the home of the beloved
But were turned back by the enemy's law and the enemy's wall

I said to myself
Perhaps it's a blessing
What will you see in Jerusalem when you visit?

You'll see everything you cannot bear
When her houses start appearing at the side of the road

On meeting the beloved, not every soul rejoices
Nor does every absence harm

If the joy of meeting ends in parting
How dangerous then is that very joy

For once your eyes have seen Jerusalem
You'll see only her, wherever you look

In Jerusalem
A greengrocer from Georgia, bored with his wife
Thinks of going on holiday or painting his house
In Jerusalem
A Torah—
And a middle-aged man from upper Manhattan
Arrives to teach young Polish men how to read it
In Jerusalem
A policeman from Ethiopia seals off a street in the market
A machine gun hangs from the shoulder of a teenage settler
A hat bows to the Wailing Wall

Blond tourists who don't see Jerusalem at all
Take photos of each other
Beside a woman who sells mint on the streets every day
In Jerusalem there are walls of basil
In Jerusalem there are barricades of concrete

In Jerusalem, jackboot soldiers march on clouds
In Jerusalem, we pray on the asphalt

In Jerusalem there's whoever's in Jerusalem
Except for you

And History turned to me, smiling:
"Did you really think your eye
Could miss all these

And see the others?

Here they are before you
They are the text
While you're a footnote or a margin
You thought, my son, a visit could draw from the face of the city
The thick veil of her present
So that you might see there what you wish?

Everyone is in Jerusalem
Except for you

And she is the deer in the distance
You've raced in pursuit of her
Since she offered her farewell glance
Go gentle on yourself – I see you fading"

In Jerusalem there's whoever's in Jerusalem
Except for you

But History, wait—
For the city has two timelines
One, foreign, complacent, steady-paced
As though sleepwalking
Another that lies in wait
Masked, cautious, silent
And Jerusalem knows herself
Ask the people there, everyone will tell you
Everything in the city has a tongue which, when you ask, will speak;

In Jerusalem the crescent moon curls tight as a fetus
Curving over its likenesses on the domes;
Through the years they've become like a father and his sons

In Jerusalem there are buildings whose stones are quoted from
Bible and Quran

In Jerusalem beauty is octagonal and blue
Supporting, gentle listener, a golden dome
That looks like, I think, a convex mirror
Containing the sky, playing with it, pulling it close
Distributing the sky, like aid in a siege
To the deserving
As the people, after the Friday sermon
Reach their hands to receive it

In Jerusalem, the sky gives herself out to the people
She protects us
We protect her
For we would carry her on our shoulders
If times were to be hard on her moons

In Jerusalem, dark marble columns rise
As though their veins were smoke
Windows, high in church and mosque,
Hold morning's hand, showing him how to paint with color
He says, "like this"
The windows say, no—
Like that—
Until they compromise
Morning is free to paint outside the threshold, but
To enter through God's Windows
He must abide by their rules

In Jerusalem there's a school built by a Mamluke
Who came from beyond the river,
Was sold at a slave market in Isfahan
To a merchant from Baghdad, who traveled to Aleppo
Gave the Mamluke to Aleppo's prince
Fearing the blueness in the Mamluke's left eye –
The Prince passed him along to a caravan heading for Egypt
Where soon, he became Conqueror of the Moghuls
And Sovereign Sultan

In Jerusalem there's a scent
That summarizes Babel and India in an herbalist's shop
At Khan Al-Zayt!
I swear, a scent with a language you'll understand
If you listen;
It says to me—
When they pitch their gas canisters at me
'Ignore them'
And when the gas has gone
That scent fills the air again, and says
'You see?'

In Jerusalem contradictions take their rest
And miracles are not strange
People touch them like bits of fabric old and new
Miracles here are handled, put to use

In Jerusalem if you shake hands with an old man
Or touch a building
You'll find etched on your palm a poem, my friend
Or two

In Jerusalem, despite the many disasters
There is an air of innocence
A breeze of childhood
A pigeon flying aloft
Declares independence in the wind between two bullets

In Jerusalem, rows of graves are lines of the city's history
Her dust the book
Everyone has passed through
For Jerusalem welcomes the faithful and the faithless
Walk through
Read her tombstones in every nation's language
Here lie the Africans and the Franks
The Kipceks and the Slavs and the Bosniaks
The Tartars and the Turks
The people of God and of Destruction
The poor and the rich
The debauched and the ascetic
Here lies everyone who's ever trod the earth
Scribe of History, why have you excluded us?

Has the city
Suddenly become
Too small?

Old man, re-write and think again

The eye closes, then looks once more

The driver of the yellow car turns north, away from the gates
And now Jerusalem is behind us
I see her in the right rear-view mirror
Her colors change in the sun and disappear

Well into tears
A smile surprises me

And says:
"Oh you who weep behind the wall, are you a fool?
Have you lost your mind?!

Let your eye not weep, you who've been dropped from the text
Let your eye not weep, young Arab, and know
That in Jerusalem there's whoever's in Jerusalem
But, in Jerusalem
I see no-one, except for you"

The Caliph and the Poet

(Excerpts from a longer text)[2]

Translated by Tamim Al-Barghouti

The first thing people knew about the Franks invading the Levant
was that flocks of eagles started throwing the ring seals of those
they'd devoured in Jerusalem across the land. The ring seals rained
over every city from Aleppo to Damascus to Cairo to Baghdad.
Each seal was inscribed with the name of its owner. This was the
incident about which Jamaluddin Hassan son of Hassan, the blind,
wrote:

The Eagles Flew
Above Baghdad
Each ring they threw
A story told

Aleppo feels
The skies are sad
It's raining seals
All made of gold

Damascus too
Woke up in shame
As people knew
Each ring had a name

---

2. This is an excerpt from a longer work that mixes historical events with
fantasy; the caliph, the judge of Damascus, Yaghisian of Antioch, Redwan of
Aleppo, Duqaq of Damascus and Zamarkal the thief are historical figures.
Usama, is Usama bin Munqidh, the 12th century knight and historian. The
judge's protests in Damascus and Baghdad, and the cannibalism committed
by the crusaders in Mi'arra are real as well. All other events and characters are
fictional. The historical account of the judge's protests is described in medieval
historical accounts, such as Ibn al-Athir's history: "al-kamel," as well as in
contemporary works such as Amin Maalouf's *The Crusades through Arab Eyes*.

And Cairo's streets
Became too narrow
As death became
Gold, round, and hollow

Tell the story of Old Baraka
The woman whom Usama's uncle
Found performing magic rituals
Near the cemetery of Shaizar
The one who was washing clothes
When the Franks laid siege
To the town from beyond the Orontes
She was right there at the banks, as if she hadn't seen them
Suddenly, she darted out, screaming at them
Flapping her clothes as if herding demons
The Franks thought she was a witch
And fled

Tell the Story of Umm Abdallah
The ghoul
Recite her poems
Reveal that she was the jurist's daughter
Say that her children kept dying
So she swallowed other people's children whole
Then called herself by her victims' names
If she swallowed Khalil, then that day she'd call herself
Umm Khalil, Khalil's mother

Tell the story of Zamarkal
The horse-thief
It is said he stole from both camps on the same day!
He used to say, "in the morning I'm a thief
By night, I am a Mujahid"

Say that the prince of Damascus tried to imprison him
In a sown up camel's hide
Seating four soldiers right on top of him
Yet he escaped

Tell the story of the man who gave birth
Just like women do—
But to a fish

Tell the story of the girl who grew her hair
Until she could hide in it
The Franks thought she was a broom
So they didn't rape her

Tell the story of those lunatics
Who came seeking a unicorn's horn in Jerusalem

Tell the story of the wise men who argued horses had wings
And who then kept searching for their fallen feathers

Talk about Hadar Al-Tout, and Saifuddin son of Qaraja
Because their names were funny

Tell of the little boy whom Usama killed
(When they were both five)
Describe how Usama saw the boy's blood
boiling

Talk about the lion that fled the ram in Shaizar
That day the soldiers laughed, but the prince didn't

Start where you first chose:
With the eagles, and the rain of seals

News came from Baghdad, that the Judge of Judges in Damascus, Fakhrul-Islam Abu Sa'd Al-Harawai, barged into the Caliph's mosque and smashed the pulpit. He then hurried to the Sultan's mosque and destroyed the pulpit there, too. Fakhrul-Islam had broken bread and eaten during Ramadan, at midday, right before Friday Prayers, while standing at the pulpit! This went beyond blasphemy and bordered on apostasy. Refugees from Jerusalem had just handed him one of the four oldest copies of the Quran, the one placed in Jerusalem by the third Caliph—the Prophet's companion, Othman. They had saved the Book. By it, they swore the Franks had killed each and every Muslim in Jerusalem, and that the blood had reached the knees of horses—even the knees of mounted horsemen. Dead bodies were intertwined like threads in a badly made rug.

When the guards came to arrest Fakhrul-Islam
He issued a fatwa
"Jihad for Jerusalem is more important than the fast of Ramadan!"
The guards could not arrest him
The revolt had begun
Damascus could not be contained
Until the prince allowed the judge to travel to Baghdad
To have an audience with the Caliph, Al-Mustazhir

The Caliph greeted the rebellious judge
He entered shaven and covered in ash, as a sign of protest
He made a speech at the Sublime Court
'Causing hearts to ache
And grown men to weep'

Yet the Caliph himself did not weep
He tried his best, but could not
He ordered a bowl of water for his ablutions
So that people would mistake
The water he washed his face in
For tears

When the meeting was done
The Caliph rode out of the palace
And found standing before him
Jamaluddin Hassan son of Hassan the poet
Hassan was singing and clapping
Surrounded by a small crowd:

All names are falling from the Sky
And still the sky is full of names
The Caliph no one ever blames
—and every bowing head salutes
Is faking tears and playing games
His beard is wet, his eyes are dry
He does not pray, yet he ablutes
So people think that he can cry

Now
Say that this poet was present in the contingent at Antioch
When the Franks laid siege to the city
Say that he stayed at the citadel with Shamsuddin, Yaghisian's son
When the Franks entered the city, and laid siege to the citadel

Three months he stayed there, witnessing the defeat of the armies
Of Mosul and Damascus.
He snuck out during the massacre that followed
Reaching Aleppo on foot

The Caliph, fearing a riot, excused Hassan's insolent song
But ordered guards to push him aside
Hassan turned to the Caliph, opened his eyes and stared at him
The Caliph said
        "Blessed be God almighty, you have regained your sight,
    Hassan!"
        "Yes, Prince of Believers, it is by your grace that I have
    regained it."

With the crowds in mind, Al-Mustazhir ordered for Hasan
A sack of gold
The poet took it, reaching into his own cloak for another
Filled with golden ring-seals
He handed this sack to the Caliph saying
And these are yours, Prince of Believers
You're their only heir now

He then slapped Al-Mustazhir's horse with the sack of coins
The horse nearly bucked the Caliph
The Caliph got angry, and said:
"Your manners were better when you were blind, old man!"
To that, Hasan answered by reciting this poem:

My blindness is precious...
You see, for when I shut my eyes
The world does not become invisible
But I become invisible to the world
You see?
I con Time with my blindness
An eye for an eye, you see?

The world shapes people's imagination
But my imagination shapes the world

My blindness is a scepter
A shepherd's staff
The days and nights are herds of sheep

If I walk down an alley
I walk down an alley of my mind
Like a tablecloth I throw my world over yours

Blind are those who trust their eyes...
Limiting knowledge to the senses
Is like moving seas in baskets

Yes, my mirage is truer than your water!
Was water real when the Commander of the Faithful wept?

Under siege, water was gold
Every night waiting, we'd man the walls
Looking for the lightning of marching swords
To bring us the rain of rescue

Three months people waited in Antioch
Screams chased the birds out of the sky
So it was made empty
From the Sea to the Euphrates
You see?

Red snow
Heads like pebbles
Catapults
Fireballs
Holy anger

And you?
You sent an army of quarrelling eunuchs
And the city fell
The conquerors marched to Mi'arra
To eat children
Mi'arra's day caused the sun to hate himself
Melting moons
Ghouls and demons were more merciful
Those marching towards Bethlehem
Celebrated over the bodies of murdered innocents

And so they marched
Duqaq of Damascus didn't stop them
Nor that madman of the north, Redwan of Aleppo
Shaizar gave them horses and other gifts
And we called for our Caliph, but he was late

We have no protector but God

Then they marched towards Jerusalem,
Then they marched towards Jerusalem,
Then they marched towards Jerusalem

At this point, the poet wept and could not go on

He cursed the Sultan, the Caliph, Redwan, Duqaq and all the
kings, one by one. The crowd believed the Caliph would order his
head off. But the judge said that the blood of a Muslim cannot be
spilt as punishment for hitting a horse with a sack of coins. And
the Vizier advised the Caliph: "Commander of the Faithful, if you
irrigate the earth with this man's blood, it will bring forth fields of
young fighting men marching against you. And if you cut off his
head, it will grow back on every man's shoulders."

The Vizier, of course, was speaking in metaphor, but the Caliph,
superstitious about things he did not understand, decided not to
execute Hassan.

He ordered another bowl of water for his ablutions
If he was not going to kill the poet
He'd best be seen moved by him
And, besides, he'd started to enjoy this ablution trick

As they all stood there together
The sky clouded up again—with eagles
And it started raining
Arabic names

The State

Translated by Tamim Al-Barghouti

A hyena attacks a herd of deer
Their hooves inscribe a thousand branches on the earth
A tree of tracks and shadows, growing fast

There's no time to think
Which doe to choose
The hyena must decide in haste
Who will live and who will die

She chooses at random

The hyena does not know the deer
There's no enmity here, no competition
If it were just another day
The hyena might have picked another

Even after the deer is dead
The hyena is incapable of explaining her choice

Yet I believe the hyena is aware
Of the balance of fear

If the herd
Runs, not from her, but towards her
They crush her, bone and all

If only the deer change the direction of their flight
They live

I also believe the herd is aware of its abilities
Yet each doe fears she'll be abandoned by her sisters
If she runs at the common foe

So she abandons her sisters

And each doe thinks the same

The deer do not fear the hyena much
They only doubt themselves
Each deer lives and dies alone
Yet, there are moments
When God is kind to the world:
A young deer darts at the hyena without thinking
The rest follow
Like rain

In moments such as these
You feel it being born
A breathing dawn
Or a baby speaking eloquently
In the cradle

I'm not writing an allegory
On Revolution
And the meek empowered
I'm simply stating a scientific fact

The hyena is weaker than her victims

And she's very much the coward

The Little Sky in My Hands

Translated by Tamim Al-Barghouti

I have my own sky, small and blue
I hold it above my head
And carry it around the world
I hold a sky in my hands!

She has all the properties of a true Sky
Aloof, yet facing downwards—
Peace between opposites
Fire and water
And stars, absent-minded
Like scattered deer

She is arrogant and shy
The wind, as usual
Is a promise and a warning

The history of my sky repeats itself
Like mornings and evenings
Yet every repetition is unique

Birds fly backwards
Longing for the lands they leave
Not for the lands they travel to
Departing their new homes
They ache also for these
Their longing stretches the horizon like a bow

In my sky, distant war-drums can be heard
Like unborn thunder at the horizon
When the sound draws near
Silence reigns and the air grows heavy

When the bombers arrive
With iron-clad, blue eyed death
My sky becomes a shelter or a tent
She tells me, with tearful eyes
All will be well
How many times before, my son
How many times before,
Have they come and gone
I have a sky in my hands

I have a sky, like *the* Sky
Young and blue
That I hold above my head

Like her bigger sister, my sky has everything:
Angels busy fixing old scales
(Revising lists of names and genealogies)
With all mankind crowded at the door
Clutching deeds and documents
(Treasures for law students—
Arguments of unrivaled eloquence)
Our entire history, what we knew
And what was hidden from us
Recounted in vivid detail

History is but our argument before God
The devil is not the accused, as we thought
But the prosecutor
Humanity prepares evidence
Calls witnesses
Hoping to prove Adam's worth
Parading events of history
Like a Syrian merchant enthusiastically displays
Chinese silk he didn't make

As if the people made their history
As if they had a choice
Noise upon noise
And in a distant corner
Resounds a melodic call for prayers

Each morning, the Jinn bring me my sky's directions
Like newspapers left at the door
This is how she talks to me
I have a sky in my hands

I have a sky, like *the* Sky,
Young and blue
I hold her up above my head
Like people hold newspapers up as protection from the sun
Like statues of Greek gods carry their temples, almost unwillingly
Where gods resemble construction workers
I raise my sky
Like the muezzin, calling for prayers
Lifts his voice, made heavy by the burdens of a long history
To a place between singing and weeping

When I'm alone at home
I hang my sky from the corners of the ceiling
And ask her to rain
She generously showers random letters
They cover the floor
I sit down, piece them together like a puzzle
Once, twice, thrice, I try
Until they make sense
I reinvent the world according to my whims
I become the second Adam
A distributor of names
I call every invasion: "flu"

(It heals on its own)
Each invader will leave, eventually
Or become one of us: language, religion, embroidery
Love for poetry

I try to turn a policeman into a human being
Since he looks like one
I will appoint a few kings and presidents I know
To new positions
As waiters, bartenders
Or offer them other honest jobs

You see, rulers have only two hands each
Most of their oppression
Is done by one subject to another
The ruled, rule
I venture to say that since Adam, we've had no rulers at all
It's just that when decent people became scarce
Bastards reveled in mutual enslavement
Hence I seek to find some use for rulers!

I re-invent old histories
I might even allow myself a forgery here and there
The Kharijites, don't rebel against Ali[3]
The Muslims revolt against Yazid[4]

---

3. The Kharijites were the followers of an Islamic sect of the seventh century
who rebelled against and then assassinated Ali, the fourth elected Caliph.
Kharijites were opposed to hereditary rule, yet their assassination of Ali
marked the end of government by election and the beginning of the hereditary
dynastic Caliphate under the Umayyads.

4. Yazid I (647-683 AD) was the second Umayyad Caliph, he ordered the death
of Hussein, Ali's son, who is also Mohammad's grandson. Yazid is seen as a
tyrant by the followers of all Islamic sects. He ruled for three years and was
succeeded by his son, Mu'awiya II.

Alqami is paraded in the market[5]
Along with all those who sold their souls
in Egypt, Syria, and Iraq
That native land of stubbornness and sacrifice

I re-arrange the maps

Of Baghdad's walls, I form a diadem of laurels
Egypt's Nile becomes a river of horses
Under angry men
The gardens of Damascus grow spears in times of war
To protect the jasmine

I might even create kind policemen, just for laughs
Set them alongside ghouls, griffins
And other curiosities

I have a sky in my hands

This of course, is immense power
I change anything I want
Holding a world that is all mine
Just above my head

---

5. Alqami was the vizier of the last Abbasid Caliph in Baghdad. He is seen as
the archetypical traitor because he opened the gates of Baghdad to the Mogul
invaders in 1258 AD allowing them to commit a 40 day long massacre that
decimated the civilian population of the city.

My close sky, like a Phoenix protects me[6]
In fact, she is the one carrying me
All around the world

Yet, as I cling to the Phoenix's claw
I say, thank you, you gave me everything
But I still need one more thing
(Quite badly I might add)
And if I die, I will have it in my will
For my children to seek

I wish I held any land, any land at all, in my hands

---

6. The bird here translated as Phoenix, is *Anqaa*, the Arabic equivalent of the Persian *Simurgh*. It shares certain features with the Greek Phoenix in that its feathers regenerate when burnt and in that it is immortal. In Arab and Persian mythology Anqaa/Simurgh protect mortal heroes, they appear from the sky when called, and carry their heroes in their claws away from danger.